Love Song

Port & Starboard

Love Song

Port & Starboard

Poems by

Ann Chinnis

Cover design by Shay Culligan
Cover image by Andrea Disario Marcusa
Wheel vector by public domain vectors on Unsplash
Author photo by Carrie Stump, Carrie Michelle Photography

ISBN: 979-8-90146-979-8
Library of Congress Control Number: 2026941004

Kelsay Books
502 South 1040 East, A-119
American Fork, Utah 84003
Kelsaybooks.com

To Connie—
my rock, my dock, my cleat, my mooring

Acknowledgments

With gratitude for Philip Schultz and my Writers Studio master class colleagues for supporting, challenging and loving me.

With deep thanks to Jeffrey Levine for his generous and wise manuscript review and thoughtful feedback.

With amazement at Luisa Igloria, loving midwife of her students' poetry.

With appreciation of Loralee Clark's keen editing skills.

The author wishes to thank the following publications in which these poems have appeared in the current or prior version:

Atlanta Review: "Wetlands"
Crab Creek Review: "Skyline"
Didcot Writers: "Ode to Home"
The Ekphrastic Review: "Time Enough"
Ex-Puritan Review: "Death"
Gyroscope Review: "A Pickle Picture," "Better Late Than Never Love Letter," "Photo 51," "Love Song: Port & Starboard"
I Can Catch Anything (Finishing Line Press, 2025): "Hippocratic Oath," "A Confusion of Senses," "How to Be a Cowgirl," "Ode to Home," "The Traps," "The Fisherman Talks Tides," "Wetlands," "Why I Work the ER on a Saturday Night"

Last Leaves: "Why I Work the ER on a Saturday Night"
Little Patuxent Review: "A Confusion of Senses"
Nostos: Poetry, Fiction and Art: "My mother's Land O' Lakes Sweet Cream butter recipe tin," "Ode on Disappointment"
Open Door: "Doxology for My Mother's Manners"
The Orchards Poetry Journal: "Limbo"
Oyster River Pages: "Disdaining her apron," "The struggle here"
Poetry Virginia 2025, Collected Winning Poem: "River Glass" Recipient of the Edgar Poe Memorial Prize, Second place—Poetry Society of Virginia
Poppet My Poppet (Finishing Line Press, 2024): "Doxology for My Mothers Manners," "Ode on Disappointment," "My mother's Land O' Lakes Sweet Cream butter recipe tin," "The Chinoiserie Wallpaper"
Pushcart Anthology, 2025: "How to Be a Cowgirl"
River Heron Review: "Nothing Fancy (for Erin)"
Rockvale Review: "Firefly," "Nacre"
Sheila-Na-Gig: "The Traps"
The Shore: "Genus Narcissus"
Sky Island Journal: "How to Be a Cowgirl," "The Chinoiserie Wallpaper"
Sledgehammer: "The Fisherman Talks Tides"
Susurrus: "Where I drift," "Leaving"

Contents

III. A Following Sea

I.
Moorings

Love Song:
Port & Starboard

—for my wife

Docking our boat,
I boast, *I've got this.*
From the dock you laugh
and say, *Take my hand.*
          It's hard
to snug a boat for every wind
and tide.

When I let the port line
droop, the starboard strains
          against its mooring. I
          secure the bow line, leaving
stern cords warring. I
          cannot tether rope to cleat
          without a fray, a chafe,
a sudden jerk that renders
our boat squirming
          in its berth like dead leaves
          hedged in tidal eddies.

I pretend
I am the captain. I bought
the nylon line
          myself.
I tied the knots
          myself.

I coiled the extra rope
into a pleasing spiral.
When I made fast
our boat, I danced
a dizzy sailor's jig—
high on self-reliance.

Our boat held tight.
When northeast breeze shifted,
our boat slammed dock and piling.
Through high tide and low tide,
flood tide and riptide,
I tied and untied and retied my knots,
          a tug-of-war,
two sets of hands
required to even up the play.
But I wouldn't have it.

This is misery,
          but it was I
who chocked
the stays, who hitched
the cleat.
          I was the one
who dangled
fenders, and I will keep
tying and untying this boat
until it sinks me.

I can cinch
the knots around the piling,
but I can't double hitch
a stubborn ship to my left wrist.
I need a second left hand
to snug that throw. I need you,
my love—my rock, my dock,
my cleat, my mooring.

The struggle here

isn't from the sea
        jagged
as a fracture—or the fringing
coral reef defying
        the sea's intrusion.
It's not from the coconut palms,
their shaggy fruits & brown fronds
        whispering endings.
No, it's the hermit crabs.

One looks at me longways
        with two fat, stalked eyeballs,
lugging a home, scrubbed of color,
cracked through its vertical
        helix. The crab short-hands
a note in the sand as it
        dodges my toes,
zags to a rockpool in this refuge of
        second chances.

It's a message I can't read—
maybe about its hand-me-down,
        upside-down shell,
or about growing old. About
finding a home that fits,
for once, or
        love again.

But now, my face reflecting
the sun’s orange, I’m getting
        sentimental.
The waves erase
        the crab’s psalm &
my wife touches my shoulder.
Let’s walk the beach.

Better Late Than Never Love Letter

There is nothing I can't do
when she puts her arms around me,
reads the Hallmark card. When my patient
from a car crash survives. When the server
tops off my wine. My life—a roll of the dice.

When you hold your hand still,
you can hear the dice rattling, like rats
in a trashcan pecking at plastic until
they scratch in unison,
and you hum along.

My wife reminds me that mice don't
roll dice—it is our fingers, and what happens
when I think my fingers are too gnarly,
but they aren't—and I quit playing.
She worries that I think I am older
than I am. That I worry about death.
About not having enough time left
in my life to write about the dice.

My friend E., with a brain tumor
kicking her ass, just butt-dialed me
again. I call her back. She picks up
her phone, *Hello,* drops it in her sofa
cushions of assisted living. The Eagles
play-off game on her TV, the volume
going up and down, up and down.

She is trying to speak to me
through the remote.

My friend Jean, a nurse who worked
with me in the ER for twenty years,
never answers my texts anymore.
When I saw the word "Saturday,"
I thought I read your text already.
I bought a dictionary of Difficult Words,
begin each text to her now with a word
we have never used in forty years
of friendship. ***Eurychoric**,*
I text her, *Want to see the Frida*
exhibit this Saturday?

Truth is, none of us can stop playing
when we are losing, or we think
we are losing, or are about to lose,
or have already lost. We throw another,
then two or three more, and our lot
becomes integers that we sum
into an umbrella, hoping we will
get less wet. I never met any patient
in the ER who wasn't drenched.

I look out the window and watch you
on your hands and knees weeding
the pink-blush drift roses

along our driveway.
It is pouring. Your head is bent
under the hood of your yellow raincoat.

You say you like to weed in the rain;
a weed's life
is a crapshoot too, so let it go out
on a high note. I will stand
at the window as the raindrops
strike glass, one by one, random
as dice, then harder and faster,
until they run together, until it's
forever that I have stood watching
your river of bright yellow
and insistent green.

Ode to Home

I hopscotched to Montserrat and snitched
        mangoes from goats. Floated
in pimiento smoke through Ocho Rios. Slept
        on a cardboard box in Belize. Dreamed
of red-eyed frogs in Honduras.
        Wove frangipanni 'round my wrist
in Nevis. I clambered up the phosphorescent
        cliffs of Cuba. Swigged Haitian anisette,
chanted psalms with waterfalls thrumming
        crags below
                into their image.

I swam with sea shells in my hair, made
        my fingers coarse sieves, let time spill
unskeined, telescoped all I knew into
        one grain of sand, which the wind stole
as her own. I became a soothsayer
        of red skies and high tides. Believed myself
a prophet of my own second coming.
        Divined my I Ching on Dominica, denied fate
exists on St. Kitts. I dealt my tarot
        in Barbados, read Thoreau under Grand Turk's
full moon. Paced the Caicos salt flats
        at midnight and bid the flamingoes
good night. I plunged into a bottomless
        asteroid lake in Barbuda. Counted stars falling
like souls in St. Vincent. Howled with monkeys
        in Costa Rica. I foraged for a home
among palm fronds, as the rain thrummed my dreams
                into its own image.

Genus Narcissus

A Girl beats her breast purple
with longing. That's how
I read it. No diagnosis. No
therapy. I love the normalcy
of it. The girl in the water
gets the Girl she wanted.
The Girl she wanted becomes
perennial. Daffodils sprout
white tepals around golden crowns,
necks stretching with passion
as deep as the pond.

When I explain my cravings
this way, no one turns away.
No one mentions
a personality disorder. Don't you
ever look in the mirror
and imagine kissing your lips?

Have you never
leaned in until your nose,
your eyes, your chin
blur, nothing remaining but lips—
pink and puckered? Have you never
marveled at four lips coming
together, how cold and calm
the mirror's surface? Have you
ever fallen in love with yourself?

And the gardener
weeds my bed,
spading red cannas, cattails,
purple water hyacinths
around me. He
smooths away my muddy
footprints, asking the water,
If I love, can I be erased?

The Chinoiserie Wallpaper

—for my grandmother

Tonight, I am thinking about your
chinoiserie wallpaper, fern green with peacocks.

We used to sleep like two spoons on the pullout
as you recited the Song of Hiawatha

and touch typed *I love you* on my shoulder. I
was six, and the man from Sears would come

door-to-door, panting satchels of wallpaper samples
up your front stairs, sweating Lucky Strikes. He

sprawled on your pull-out. *What look are you going for—*
Country Inn, Garden Club? He pegged you

for *Patriotic,* since you worked on Capitol Hill.
But you traveled once to Brazil,

wanted *Exotic.* I thought the wallpaper
the height of glamor, out of Reader's Digest.

And when you bought bedsheets almost
matching the wallpaper, I couldn't sleep, traced

my index finger along the peacock's plumage,
the pagodas and pandas. You overflowed with laughter,

opened your umbrella in the foyer, grabbing my
hand and your purse as we headed to your office

on Saturday. How is it that time has not faded
the paper, caused it to peel from the wall?

As I pass from breath, into death, will I step past
the pull-out in your living room one more time,

will you take my hand along that path by the garden—
the one by the pond where the koi sleep under the lotus,

where the egret is singing, where you told me
you'd wait, if we were ever separated?

How to Be a Cowgirl

First, don't call yourself Cowgirl.
Shove your sockless feet
in the red leather boots from last summer.
Ignore your brother's laughter.

Then go find a pony.
Snake through a break in a fence,
daring the brambles to stop you.
Sing towards the pasture like you are a siren,

and your Ulysses—any friendly pony. Cinch
the strap tighter on your red straw hat
for lift-off. Grab a handful
of mane and fling yourself

onto destiny's haunches. Bow
your head to the field before you,
the fescue, big bluestem, dogtooth violet
grander than any garden in town.

Read your fortune in the galena that glitters
through the Missouri red clay.
Let the Queen Anne's lace reveal
your true fate: its cluster of hundreds

whisper the words to a poem about your future
as a pilot, or a doctor or a forest ranger.
Your holster and cap-gun will be your courage—
tested at sunset, in thunderstorms, by the bark

of a stray. Lay your face on the neck
of your pony and smell how her sweat is sweeter
than peppermint in your Christmas stocking. Notice
how the clomp of her hooves on limestone

has more purpose than most people you know.
Ride with unbridled ambition
across the meadow, like a hive of bees.
Back home on the porch, you stare at the train tracks,

counting the minutes, 'til the 10PM from St. Louie
rattles your glass with its whistle.
Before you, watch the sycamore peeling bark
that's too tight for its stretch. Above you,

be humbled by the sapphire sky with no limits.
Below you, relax into the sway of the pony.
Believe that your pony knows where,
one day, you'll be going.

My father taught me how to fish

even with his polio.
He'd sit to cast because he couldn't stand,

flick his left hand out the window
of a fast-moving Buick, right wrist

on the wheel, and snag a full-bellied bass
one county over. Sitting on the bank

of the Withlacoochee River, before the sun
burns off the night, all I need are my lures

and the tide. Strung out in the grass
they look dead, but when I skim them

across the moss, the yellowtail jigs
and the red-topped twirlers bounce,

and I can catch anything: a glint,
a memory, a ripple widening in the wind.

When my father crossed the international
date line on the USS Little Rock

right before polio caught him, he trolled
'round Cape Horn. All the fish turned back

their clocks—all the dorado, all the tarpon—
because they knew their days were numbered.

The ensigns wrote home: *We are headed*
to Rio, gorging on mahi. They dated

their postcards tomorrow. And the fish
swam in reverse back to their past. That's
why I sit, while the tide runs.

Fishing line

is fickle—scoffs at boxes; tackle is stowed
with surgical precision—each swivel, hook,
lure & sinker divining fishergirl's upstream
journey. At six, bloodworm on treble hook.
Clenching the rod's cork grip. Her father's
hand steadying hers. Push-button reel singing
salt-water & steel. Fishergirl gasps, two eyes
peering from one side of her fish—
        I can catch anything.

Fishing line is happy jigging cattails;
tackle knows its place in Walmart—
red-topped twirler on aisle five
by filet knives. At sixteen, winging her skiff
through a million silver spoons scooping sunlight.
Casts crank bait where birds work the water—
        I own this river.

When reel releases drag, fishing line squeals
across the water—triumphant free-spool. Tackle
feels safest wrapped in plastic, heeding physics.
At twenty-six—after an ER night shift—replaying
sick patients under her eyelids, naps under blue-gray
clouds that swirl like shorebirds. Trolls
choppy water with a yellow popper—
        I can save anyone!

Fishing line—erratic at best—should
not be stowed with tackle, when off-duty
must be spooled, prepared for strike or run,
braced for break or backlash. At thirty, drifting
in moonlight. The death of her patient. She hurls
her stethoscope into the breeze of crab and diesel—
I am a failure.

Fishing line knows joy when weighted, unspooled
to depths, beseeching tackle, "Scrape the rocks,
snag some seaweed." Is not ashamed to crack
the river's glass, return with bait unnibbled.
Fisherwoman sings in braided nylon—
I can tell you what it's like to hit the bottom.

Doxology to My Mother's Manners

My mother's manners are an apology for her Ozark
roots—thank you notes nibbed on monogrammed cards,
    swift and gift specific, serious as a Vanderbilt

gilding her audience, but home-spun too, penning barefoot
as she yarns you about her one-room school, windows rattling
    from the train to St Louie, the kids waving

like crazy to a hazy face, counting boxcars. Her manners
are a ruse. She never said *stupid* unless delivered as catechism;
    Stupid is as stupid does, each time I back

into the same mailbox. As steadfast as her Aqua-Net hair,
my mother's manners are more resolute than her starched
    sheets. Even when I'm grown, move from home,

she stashes my coat on her bed with the guests', sends me
off with the rest, after sherry, saying, *Don't be a stranger.*
    They are a lasso of truth—how she offers

me punch in a crystal cup, lulls me into spilling my guts.
What do you think of your father's new wife?
    My Mother's manners are a bribe—

German Chocolate cakes baked from scratch, coconut and
fingertip grated into icing, delivered in my Pinto
    to Lenten Luncheons when she campaigned

for church Senior Warden. Her manners are a Trojan horse
sporting a periwinkle beret down K Street to Vestry meetings,
        me in red Keds, us scheming to upend creeds

on ordaining women priests. They are a sucker punch
in black leather gloves from October through March,
        not one day later, pinching my arm when I half-kneel

in church. Before she takes the dais, she puts herself down—
Good-Old-Wishy-Washy-Mom. I think she's eating
        from the palm of everyone's hand. A battering ram,

she clears her throat, raps her gavel: *the Distinguished Deputy
from Delaware is Out of Order. Please sit down.* Her manners
        are trotlines set for the vote with silver butter press

on the left, salt cellar—right: her bait, pounds of shrimp
Thermador (lemon removes the stench from your hands)
        swallowed hook, line and dogma by her guests.

My mother's manners are a psalm, a call to action.
I end her battle hymn in benediction. The last train
        from St. Louie echoes up the tracks.

A distant whistle. Three-short. One-long.

                                        Unanswered calls.

A Pickle Picture

My brother texted me a thumbs-down emoji.
        No more
pictures of our mother in her blue
cotton muumuu, sautéing button mushrooms
while reproving Bishops in two columns
on her cookbook flyleaf:
        Pro Ordination of Women & Con.

I am still grieving, he texted.
        No pictures
of her justice speeches typed on onionskin paper
or a picture of her file card printed in fountain pen,
        "Shrimp Thermador for Forty,"
culinary coercion for her political missions.
Which meant no more pictures of me,
because while my mother typed
brave addresses about oppression, I rested
my head on the floor by her desk, adoring
        the stubborn thunk
of her Smith Corona's manual carriage return,
picturing myself in her image,
a gentle anarchist too—even one day,
an ER doctor. Instead, I sent him
        a pickle picture,
not even that black and white picture

from ’76, Rev. Jeannette Piccard kneeling—
her ordination at sixty-nine—first female
Episcopal minister, my mother beaming.
It wasn’t that picture. This was a picture
        of a perfectly pickle-shaped pickle,
fished with metal tongs from a vat of brine
        at 7-eleven by my mother
in her high heels & leather gloves & periwinkle beret.

No, this was a picture
        of a companionable pickle
on the front seat of our mother’s
Country Squire station wagon with faux wood trim
that she drove city to city, shaming
her non-inclusive church with speeches
she typed on her Smith Corona.
        A patient pickle in the passenger seat,
waiting for me to finish field hockey practice.
        A bashful pickle in a wax paper bag,
like my mother, disguised as disarming.
        A charming pickle—like my mother’s Ozark yarns—
making lemonade from a vinegar day.
        A powerful pickle overwhelming my mother’s
perfume with onion & garlic.

The day I quit the field hockey
team, after warming the bench for another season,

my mother, upon seeing my defeated face
slouch into the car, handed me the wax bag
with the pickle. My mother, plucking our pickle-penny
off the dashboard—
          like she did every day—
slid the coin into my palm,
          Heads, you bite first. Tails, it's me!

I Loved Your Birthday

—for my mother

By your August twelfth birthday,
the cicadas were brazen

and kept us awake most nights,
while the tree frogs' song was stifled

by the boil of the river. But the peaches!
The peaches, preened in pink—

a chorus line fuzzing the window sill,
facing the creek where the cattails

could not even breathe. You
billowed about the kitchen

in your blue cotton muumuu, and I kissed
your damp forehead saying

you looked like a Chesapeake Bay clipper,
magnificent sails unfurled.

When we were done churning,
we stood in the kitchen

and ate peach ice cream with our fingers,
dropping chunks of gold

on the floor, me dripping summer
down the front of my bathing suit

as I toasted you with melting ice cream:
Praise be to vellum—defensive hairs

of peach, joy of boy's chin.
Praise pitted seed—cling

or freestone. Praise the flesh of both.
How do we cradle that which made us?

Praise the stem, our mooring. Praise be
the soft, brown bruise—our proof of living.

Narration of Medicine

Like a breezeless creek feeding the river,
the hospital's sliding glass door
startles me with our faces. Fluorescent lights
speckle the flesh of nurses' aides
        heaving mottled patients
against an unseen current. My hand cupped
in yours, I ask you where the patients are going,
        because I love to hear you,
my uncle, narrate your house of medicine:
        Radiology, lab, the intensive care unit.
        They all need something quickly.

Bleach stings my eyes where the orderly
mops up a puddle. You lean down, explain
        that *death prowls these halls*
when the moon smiles on the marsh,
but sleeps when rain cracks the river's glass.
        You place the earpieces
of your stethoscope in my ears
and rest the bell on your chest.
        Beloved niece, healers hear with our hearts.

A foreign language I heard in your heart beat.
I longed to speak it. We stop outside
        the cafeteria, listen for souls
entering and leaving—softly
as cattails asleep in the moonlight.

This evening, as we walk towards the ER,
where your patient is in labor, the healers
        in white are egrets wading
through linoleum scuffed the color
of low tide. Families in the waiting room
        buzz like diesels of deadrise
fishing boats clawing for oysters. I imagine
the loggerhead floating in the river,
        its shell cleaved
by an outboard engine.

Why I Work the ER on Saturday Nights

—for my Uncle John

On a Saturday night, I draw
the short tongue depressor to fix
the knife fight's loser. All I need
are my fingers and thread. I turn
the lights low, close one eye, listen
to the fascia chant to its muscle,

smell where the Cupid's bow longs
for the lip, feel the chin's cleft,
bereft for its jaw. With my needle
I can make anything better than new:
a drooping spirit, a yawn,
the sun's orange rising
through the ambulance doors.

This is the truth:
When my Uncle John, who taught
me how to suture, sat on the bank
of the James River, his buddy
snagged a fat catfish, the barb
mauling its mouth. My uncle shut
his good eye, plunged his hand
in the bucket, sutured the gape,
and set the fish free. When all the catfish
tumbled down the falls, hit the rocks silly,
they lipsticked their whiskers,
and waved to my uncle,
then plunged in deep silver.

II.
Narrow Channels

Wetlands

When I think of home, I think of our sinking backyard—
        a mangle of wetlands, the tangle of marsh
at the foot of the mound where my father built
        a house on the Rappahannock River in Virginia,
because wetlands were cheap, and he loved to crab.
        You live underwater when you spend all day
baiting traps, trapping crabs, tripping over gills and claws

        shaken from trap onto dock, slipping on crab slime.
Summers were one slipup after another, the hoisting
        of our haul, my father and his steel pot bubbling,
blue crabs boiling blue, me pitching crabs back
        in the creek, crabs skittering to freedom, me
in hot water again. My father's disappointment, *They're*
        escaping. My envy of the crab's sideways flight.

Tonight, it is too blue cold for blue crabs, yet I see
        those summers. The splintered dock. The rusted traps.
The tangled rope. My father. The barnacles. The stars.
        My father would spin me under the night sky.
Where is Cancer? he'd quiz, each constellation
        his catch. *Look at Pisces*, he commanded. At dinner,
he said a grace that began, *Lord, thank you*

        for this meal, meaning this catch, *his* catch, bless
our catch of the day, catch me if you can, my father
        praying with his bait-your-trap-now voice, *There is*
a girl here who hath five barley loaves and two crabs,

and the two crabs she divided among all, and they all
did eat—all five thousand. His prayer caught
on the wooden mallet that cracked open the claws,

the crabs crushed, the hot pot boiling over.
Reeking soil, floating fish heads, my T-shirt
molding, jellyfish stinging my arms, my father
with his cigar singing, *We are anglers, Annie, anglers,*
my hair stiff with salt water, summers long, winters
lonely, sun like thunder, dock like train tracks that stop
where the creek runs fast to the bay.

River Glass

Sea Ray 360, Bayliner Bowrider,
        Boston Whaler 480. Craving
those names—mathematical-hot,
        like Tabasco glazing a fiberglass

eagle—I wander the aisles
        of the winter boat show & stroke
cold bows of V-hulls, pontoons with my open
        palms. But I love the heat

of an engine too—a fast, fast
        4-stroke dual-outboard slicing
the Chesapeake Bay like a shark's
        fin. I cinch my Ray Bans

tight to my head & hammer
        the swells in a C-Hawk 250,
its Bimini top in a sexy shimmy.
        I'd like to slide slick as a minnow

into the silky berth of a 32-foot
        Chris Craft cabin,
& after I worked 24-hour
        shifts in the ER—not to forget

the sky's sapphire—
        I'd nap on the river
in my second-hand Glastron,
        a 16-foot runabout my patient

sold me cheap when he broke
        his ankle hopping into the cockpit.
I'd sleep while seagulls screeched
        & the salt water slapped the hull.

Beyond all others, I loved my
        first boat, a ten-foot fiberglass dingy,
my father bought me. *Head on out now,*
        while I smoke a cigar. A bribe

not to shame the killing schemes
        concocted with his duck hunting
buddies—painting a landlocked aluminum
        Skeeter to look like a cornfield.
You see finite things from a boat
        in a field. From a boat
on the water, long necked geese
        whiffle in for a landing while heart-shaped

loggerhead turtles paddle
        and U-Hauls bounce on the blue
suspension bridge above you. Rain cracks
        the river's glass as lightning splits

the horizon & you count the seconds
        until you yelp from the thunder,
thinking this time, you are going to die.
        But I love the feel of the wet,

metal throttle when I lay it down
        hard, the salt water stinging my eyes
while I gun it home to the dock. Even now,
        when I grab a wet mooring line

or hear fiberglass smack a creosote piling,
        it feels like I am fatherless.

Where I drift

now, is never quiet;
cordgrass creaks with salt marsh

periwinkles. Blue crabs click
at oyster shells scrapped

on the river bank. Beyond
Calf Pasture Point, the current

belches past cattails
to Church Prong Inlet, its chime

summing the hours. In brown
shallows of Dead and Bones Cove,

I loop my boat's line around
a loblolly pine, its bark scaling

praises to yellowed needles.
An Atlantic croaker cracks

the river's glass for a breath
of air in August. Virginia Bluebells

croon; moth hummingbirds seduced
by their music. I breathe

a salt and sky-blue symphony.
As a girl, I caught a spot fish here

for my father. Raced it home
to him. Dredging my silvered gift

from the bucket, he shook his head.
Too small to eat, as he tossed it

into the creek. The speckled stiffness
struck the water with the sound of waves

lapping a fiberglass hull, fingers
tapping an empty bucket.

Headless

The obstetrician's scalpel got me going
like a red-hot poker. Through

my mother's womb, he sliced
the back of my neck.

Our blood mingled
with disinfectant

on the delivery room floor.
She cried, sanctifying

my arrival. Headless saint
on Salome's platter,

I am chastened
by the knife's violation.

I lie still as plates. Quiet
as a blanket. My mouth

sealed like an unaddressed
envelope. I am no more

welcome than cicadas
in May. I belong less

than the red fox in my yard,
its young clucking

in a hard den. I am shy.
I have no more desire

to speak than the pink ribbon
in the girl's curls. When asked

to talk, my fingers flutter
like night moths to the base

of my skull, longing to nest
in my fat, pink scar. I listen:

a gale rages
under my fingers.

The moon slats silver
through my bedroom shutters.

I open my mouth. A dog bark
echoes across the creek.

My mother's Land O'Lakes Sweet Cream butter recipe tin

rests on sacred ground where orange Formica nestles
gold Hot Point range: recipes typed on white file cards.

Pam's Episcopal Punch: In a large punch bowl, combine one quart orange ice with 1 bottle vodka and 2 quarts chilled ginger ale. Add a block of ice when the first guest arrives. Serves 15–20. Typically, 10.

Mad chemist, my mother fumigates her punchbowl with Wright's Silver Polish until the kitchen reeks of diesel. She punishes the ladle with grey flannel until every print is lifted, extracts a just-washed punch glass from my soapy hand, spins it in the sun, prisms crystal into color, her laugh a champagne flute clinking.

Never by the rim, so thin and prone to break. See how water spots cast rainbows?

She washes them again. You always know where you stand. As each churchly guest arrives, she exchanges overcoat for punch glass. Would that every daughter be her aide de camp, catch her wink as she flings you their wrap. Your bed a coat rack, a bivouac. Your room, a proving ground. Me her private, privy to her sortie righting a hallowed wrong.

Land O' Lakes certified sweet cream butter, Minneapolis, Minnesota, scores 93 butter points; you can read that on the tin. My mother has no truck with butter that is not FINE, SWEET, and CLEAR. Should butter or daughter fail to please, there is the crush of sterling butter press, the welt of her silence.

So disappointed how you throw yourself away.

You always know where she stands. *Spa Vichyssoise Soup: Serve very cold,* with a hit man's sangfroid. Her frustration mounts with *Williamsburg Cheese Straws.*

I have never had much success with cutting into strips. Use a whiskey jigger to press into biscuits and place a pecan in the middle.

What daughter hasn't bucked her mother's blade, only to face a jigger in her middle? My mother unveils her piece de resistance:

Shrimp Thermidor for 100: 40 lbs. of cooked shrimp, mushrooms, flour, milk, butter, salt, cheese, and sherry. Or white wine, if preferred.

You could bask in 40 shelled pounds of her fierce approval.

You have left not a shred of vein on the shrimp; Eat one, my love, go ahead!

Sterno stews under the chafing dish; both of us warming, chafing.

They will remember the Thermidor when the vote is called.

Mamie Eisenhower's Million Dollar Fudge raises her guests' white flag of surrender—marshmallow cream creeping from warm cocoa center, meandering around obstacles of pan.

Take a lesson in concession, my stubborn dear.

With a straight edge, in fountain pen, my mother ruled the last card for me in her Land O' Lakes Sweet Cream Butter recipe tin. It is otherwise blank, not penned as an invitation—more drawn like a gauntlet.

On Disappointment

We rocked facing hunched
        pinyons. Potted
saguaro cactus wobbled
        on cobalt tiled table.
We wanted desert—
        the Red Rock before us,
like a blow torch the welder ignited:
        sunset.

To mothers and daughters,
        we toasted—you
in black Ferragamo shoes,
        a two-piece navy knit suit,
your Chanel handbag on the terra-cotta;
        me in cut-offs, a ballcap. A
sand etched sliding-door, sun bleached
        mesa print bedspread.

Dinner, your camera snapped
        my tangled hair,
defiant wildness in my eyes—
        taxonomy
of an unknown species.
        You inhaled
the desert willow, your face
        a poppy closing.

Next morning, I wrote you a poem.
        My pen plumbed
depth of canyon, slide
        of rock
blazing yellow, red, and orange
        lichen crust
down our chasm. We are losing
        each other
at different hours in this smudged
        vortex of sage

and quartz. I packed the car.
        You disappeared
down the path, returned humming—
        a yellow fiddleneck
blooming behind your ear. The sun
        seared the asphalt
as we walked, hands locked,
        towards our car,
steadied on the edge of a gully.

Sweeping

Why don't we notice,
when we leave home again,
our mothers saying once more,
Honey it's late. Heads
leaning through the driver's side
window breathing another story
about a speech they gave or
their sick patients? Why don't we
notice, when we put our car
in reverse and they grab
the broom, that the steps
are already impeccable?

We wave our left arm
like crazy out the window.
Our mothers grow smaller
in the rear-view mirror,
and the space between us
grows bigger. They
disappear into years. Sweeping,
unlike cleaning, a gesture
so tender—if you thought about it—
you could never back your car out
of the driveway.

Is this sweeping
mere distraction, a fidget
to quiet the mind? Or might

this swishing be a bit of theater,
reassurance from mother to child
that this leaving—it's business
as usual. Before we put our cars
in reverse, with angled or standard,
push broom or whisk, our mothers
sing a hymn.

The front door locking.
The porch spotless.
The back of our heads slowing
for the stop sign at the corner.

Bashful

My mother in bed
when I came home from school.
Hush, said my grandmother,
She's had a breakdown.
Your mother has always been
so quiet.

Being born bashful,
I can describe how crayons
smell when you chose to stand
facing the wall in school,
choked on your words,
warm wax mingled
with sweat of other kids coloring.

Kneeling over my bed reading,
the guests' laughter downstairs,
the clink of ice in highballs
intrigued and terrified me

like rattlesnakes. In high school,
I was attracted to spiny succulents,
spare and defensive that—unlike
the flamboyant tree by the chapel—
did not annoy me. I love the opaque
and mutable of bashful.

In college I chose
friends who were loud and drank
heavily. They forgot I was there.
That's why we got along.

In med school, the thrust of my arm
through a sleeve, my white coat
coaxing my mouth to open. I am
a doctor, trained to speak diagnoses.
I wrap bashful in white
when I save lives.

After a 24-hour shift in the ER,
Doc, quick, room three, your
asthmatic patient is coding!
Doc, can you talk to the family?
Adrift on the river, the drone
of deadrise boats laden
with oysters, the song of terns
from the bridge's trusses. Bashful
and I nap on the river.

As I write, bashful and happy
rest in the sunlight
that splinters the prism
dangling from my window. I listen
for the thud of an ice cube falling
alone into a plastic bin, one lilac
branch tapping my window.

Disdaining her apron

and *The Joy of Cooking,* my mother
nudged a champagne flute
from the top shelf of the china cabinet,
filled it halfway with Perrier-Jouët,
and tendered it to me, whispering
into my ponytail, *Every twelve-year-old girl*
should learn how to hold her liquor.

We drank to '68,
to change, to each other.
While toasting my mother
for the fourth or fifth time,
giddy from the fragile rim
that clinked my
teeth, the bubbles surprising my tongue,
a suspense of fizz in my nose,
I shattered the flutes in our hands.
Plucking shards off the counter,
mopping the floor, laughing,
we rang in the New Year
on our knees.

Running through our house
in white socks, the floors
were blameless. Cinnamon nested
in the spice rack between bay leaves
and cumin. I often surprised my mother's
Dixie Cups of vodka

behind the Smith-Corona
        in her attic office
where she typed fiery speeches.

There is no map from Bedlam
        that brings you all the way back,
wrote Anne Sexton, the same age
        as my mother. Bedlam—
the abyss of an accomplished woman.
        Six years later, Anne Sexton
was dead, and my mother, sick
        of drinking, committed
herself—a locked room
        disguised as ambition's cure.

My first year of college
        the weeks never passed
fast enough for Sunday: the hum
        of the highway, the smell of bleach
in the hospital lobby, our one-hour visits.
        My mother gifting me
another basket she crafted, *Tell me*
        about your classes.
Yellow tulips braving blossom. Our fingers
        unlinking, my car door ringing closed
like a New Year's toast.

Hippocratic Oath

I would never have been a doctor
if I hadn't commanded my friend
Betty Jean to climb on the basement
table. If I hadn't told her—

You are going to feel worse
before I make you feel better.

If I hadn't pinched the baby fat
above her knee until it welted.
If I had ceased when she pleaded—

Stop, now make it better.

At six, when my parents were fighting
and leaving, leaving and fighting,
I learned that soothing feels best
when preceded by suffering.
If I hadn't placed a Band-aid on
Betty Jean's knee, she would
never have hugged me. That hug,
after forty years in the ER—

I'm still trying to earn it.

Photo 51, Showing the X-ray Diffraction Pattern of DNA

Alone in the back row of cell biology
classroom forty years ago, I wept upon seeing
Photo 51—Rosalind Franklin's 1952
image in black and white,
her fifty-first X-ray of DNA.
A grainy X rippled like a creek
in the breeze, a twisted
ladder of sugar—every rung a pair
of two bases. DNA coiled into a self:
how soft my touch, how deeply I listen,
if I am introverted, tall or myopic. DNA
weaving my love of words that glint
like trout, break the river's
glass in the still of August, lift
like a night heron.
In the DNA's spiral, I saw the relentless
geometry of pine cone scales, the logarithmic
whorl of a nautilus shell, an ear's helix. The DNA's
lace traced the corkscrewed pain of my
shyness: its exquisite symmetry a parable
about inevitability, about finding
quiet or beauty in the tiniest things. I was
overcome by hope—or was it a preponderance
of data—that I was not as flawed
as I thought, and maybe
even glorious.

Nacre

Craving the smell   of dock in the morning
creosote deck boards   baked into stink
of salt, mothballs   after an ER night shift
I shake the oyster shell   snared by the current
from my rusted crab trap   A young ER doctor, I imagine
the shell's missing half   burnished by the river's
bottom. If I find it,   can I mend
its hinge, restore   the oyster halves
to wholeness?   Razored fringe, its empty lining
my shell reeling teal   to pink in sunrise.

Saturday night   while I suture his hand
mangled by a propeller   an oysterman and I
talk healing.   *Doc, when an oyster*
is shucked, its attachment   *to shell is gashed,*
leaving a scar of yellow,   *purple, even black.*
The waiting room full: another gunshot wound
the baby is blue.   I drink yesterday's coffee
fluorescent lights flicker   night feels forever
the tide ebbing   crab trap gaping
my oyster shell   its wounded beauty.

Skyline

—after Anne Sexton, "Letter Written on a Ferry
While Crossing Long Island Sound"

I am pleased to see that the bark
on our pin oak is curling.
I am back home
and I am remaining home
and I have buried your belongings
in boxes, as I intended to do
and I have not turned back
and I am sitting on the back deck of my house,
that was our house.

Love,
everything is different,
and nothing is different.
The tree branches are a stilled clock.
The tree is our nakedness without
pretense,
now twisted with
unreachable distance.

Skin. This is
my skin: the West Virginia wind
feels wet on my skin. Dead leaves
fall with wet clatter
onto my wet house slippers. My deck
says enough of this racket. Fine,

I say to myself.
I will keep quiet.

In my neighbor's yard I see a
dachshund prying up dandelions
like a carpenter, her nose
excavating the dirt as intently
as a detective glued to a clue.
The rain falls in gray sheets
and swamps her snout
in mud. Almost drowned,
I see the true form
of the dachshund,
twenty-six ribs, a skull
and a pelvis.

Even though I am heartbroken,
let this dachshund
leave behind her paws, her bent ears
in this asphyxiating mud,
let her arch and glide with
webbed feet, dorsal fin,

across the yard where all the
trees were cut down, where there

are no azaleas; let her set sail,
her mouth open, pink tongue
a rudder; cutting the water sharply,
without remorse. When she arrives
let her call to me,
I'm home.

Time Enough

—to Alma Thomas, who exhibited solo at
the Whitney at the age of 81

I never see azaleas, Miss Thomas,
that I don't think of you, wedged
between canvas and bed,
broken hip mending, spinning out
        scarlet strokes
that float across thirteen feet
of empty. One hundred fifty-eight inches
of "Red Azaleas Singing and Dancing Rock and Roll
    Music"—
you, feeling twenty inside,
        wanting more time.
When I look at my page again, Miss Thomas,
my words shimmy, pinhole bright light,
ignite with ruby, daub chunky green. I am
seeing my pages as if from the moon:
        anew, beautiful.

But what about the voice at my desk
        that says
I am too damn old? That woman
in my poetry workshop who smirked
when she read this and asked me
        what in the world
I think I could tell you.
When I turned my back to her
and spoke, Miss Thomas,
it was the truth. I said,
        Everything.

III.
A Following Sea

Firefly

—for my mother

In hospice, when I droppered the morphine under her
tongue, my mother closed her eyes and scanned a
faraway night

for signs of her Ozark homeplace. She was surprised by
the fireflies which, in the Missouri night, favored
silver and white

Northern Lights, but dark hadn't fallen, and she couldn't
yet hear porch rockers creaking, or her mother's
laughter. Where

were the crickets? When she set out past the white
hollyhock, towards the fireflies, the creek grew
brighter. The bridge

out of town had waited eighty years for her to cross back
over. When she stood on the bridge and cupped a
firefly, she was

once more, my mother—not the sad woman who, after
my father left us, sat in the attic typing speeches
supporting justice

for women. I would lie with my head next to her desk
and close my eyes to the sound of her Smith-Corona,
the strike

of the keys mechanical, the swipe of the carriage return
furious—my life imprinted with her loneliness and
vengeance

that I took as my own anger and detachment. Once
more, she became the mother who unscrewed my
canning jar lids,

freed my fireflies, spun in her white cotton nightgown
beneath their breathtaking beauty with a cry that
might have

embarrassed me but didn't, letting me know there was
more to our lives besides the empty in our attic. It
made me believe we

were overflowing. It wasn't the bridge she needed, not in
the least—she had traveled the world giving
speeches. The steady

fireflies did what she loved them for—they reappeared
every night to remind her of home. She didn't feel
the shame of her

strokes, could say "firefly" as she held it, intrigued by its
blinking—a harbor light flashing safe passage.

Watching the fireflies flick in a cluster—when the night was so big, and they were free to fly anywhere—she again felt the joy

of her aunts setting the old oak table, hanging their aprons on the backs of their chairs, laughing. I sat by her bed holding

her hand, and my mother opened her eyes, as if to tell me she made it home before night fell.

Why I Drove My Mother's Revlon *Cherries in the Snow* Lipstick to Galena, Missouri

Because my mother never climbed a podium to deliver a speech without a fresh coat of Revlon *Cherries in the Snow* lipstick.

Because when she broke down, she applied her red lipstick and drove those twelve hundred miles back to her homeplace, Galena, across the Y-Bridge.

Because I rented a white Chrysler 300 to drive her red Revlon lipstick in a blue Igloo cooler the twelve hundred to Galena.

Because I leaned over her casket & applied the red lipstick to her lips the best I could, wanting it to look like her doing, but aware that it didn't.

Because I thought to place the lipstick in her hand before they closed the casket.

Because I am never clear about where I begin & my mother ends, I took her red Revlon *Cherries in the Snow* lipstick from her hand &
I kept it.

On the day Karla Hayden is fired

having stashed my dead grandmother's flatware
under my bed for thirty-four years;
I am selling her silver. The dealer's
LED scale beams its weight blue
on my chest: metallic & criminal.
When the dealer
tenders me money—unlike
when we snuggled on her pull-out sofa,
two soup spoons silvered by DC streetlights
as my granny touch typed
our conversation on my shoulder—

today, I no longer recognize myself
as her granddaughter.
I have forgotten so much. How many
7" iced tea spoons? The color of tarnish.
I sniff the Smithsonian dishtowel
padding her flatware in its walnut box.
Is that her Joy perfume?
The note on pink paper, embossed
"House of Representatives,"
where she worked as a secretary,
tucked under cutlery she scrapped
vacations to buy,
the "Queen Anne Williamsburg"
pattern bearing her first granddaughter's

first name, *To my beloved granddaughter,*
when I pass, from her Ever-Lovin' Gran.

Today, I am selling my grandmother's
flatware because I gave up hope
that safe places—
like the Library of Congress—
for books and people will survive; me, at six,
in shiny red shoes, my granny whispering,
Hush now. This is a church for books.
Hard chairs in the main reading room.
Our hands resting on the wood desk's
cool surface—her veined left
over my right, my eyes tearing
as I looked up at the dome,
Human Understanding
lifting her veil. I understood
that one day,
I would have to live
          without my granny.

The dealer says
he will blowtorch her silver. I will hide
the five hundred dollars under my bed.

Until my guilt melts in a crucible. Until
I am cast one last time
as her granddaughter.

How to Grieve Your Dying Friend

Don't think like a doctor,
in odds and timelines. She has lived with her brain tumor

for fifteen years. Choose a full moon. One with a name.
Like Strawberry, Buck or Sturgeon. On the night

of your grieving, do not text her as you did for decades—
Full moon rising! for she can no longer read.

When you sight the first star of the night, work your feet
into your flip flops and walk to the water's edge.

The breakers will pummel your ankles. All things
anchored must be hammered deeper. Picture

the plate your grandmother painted with purple grapes
and brown quail—the beauty of the plate's jagged glue.

When the silver moon fingernails over the horizon,
step back from the water. Steady yourself.

It won't be long now. If you can—
silence your words, *This cannot happen,*

If you must weep, weep. Now it's time to look
at the stars and dream her husky laugh.

Things of joy—you hear her speak them with a voice
that reminds you of colors. The orange butterfly bush

in her yard. Fireworks on a clear night
over the Monongahela River. The yellow and blue

dragonfly tattoo on her ankle before she began
brain radiation. Repeat them aloud in the night,
repeat them until the next full moon.

Nothing Fancy (for Erin)

Like a dragonfly may you find beauty in your journey.
—Erin, after a six pack

I.

Don't make it this fancy
& you tossed Vinnie your phone—

the first picture you found
after your biopsy—dragonfly wings

veined in jade, a woman's face
carved in green chalcedony, asleep

as her bust fights its way
out of the mouth of a griffin &

Vinnie, the strip mall tattoo artist,
who owns the ABC store next door,

not a patch of flesh on his hands
un-inked. *Yeah, that's a Lalique.*

Pretty classy. You just want
a dragonfly, right?

You held tight your lighted cigarette
and a warm Corona with lime

while you climbed on the table
& when the ink gun buzzed your calf

you said, *Wait. Make it say*
"Let the Journey Begin."

II.

It's night shift of a home football game &
the ER waiting room is standing-room only.

ER manager, you plant yourself at the sliding doors
in your navy heels, your hose with a run

up the back of each leg. You boom *Welcome!*
as you hand condoms to students, cups of water

to toddlers. I sprint past you on my way
to suture a face & grumble,

Do you have to be so hospitable?
At 6 am, you are rubbing your bunions

& I ask if you still want to be a Walmart Greeter
one day. *Making people happy is what I do best.*

Your shift over, you step out
the ambulance doors into the darkness.

III.

We're hiking along a stream
under a white umbrella of hemlock,

when your doctors say you have
six months, your scalp incision healed

& your radiation burns faded
& you are talking

strategy—how to make the patients
happy & like a doctor, I am saying *Uh huh,*

& counting your minutes. You are
quiet & I turn to watch you—plaid shorts,

a puffy, red parka, one blue Keds in each hand—
sloshing barefoot across the cold river rocks. You

pause on a flat stone to consider the outline—
pine-green wings inked on your calf, two slate

antennae sensing the pulse of your muscle
& you laugh with the abandon of a great blue heron

lifting in flight. *Chinnis. Let's shut up*
and smell the hemlock!

IV.

Beloved friend, you showed me what
real friendship is by loaning me

your rose-colored glasses—
when it rained on the Fourth or our Coronas

were warm. When our patients grew testy
from waiting. After my mother suffered

one more stroke. You would say this
more simply than I can, with some

pithy quote from the bathroom wall
of a Pittsburgh diner

where you are in true love
with the pepperoni rolls—moaning

Mm, Mmmm, Mmmmm, with each mouthful,
saying, *Life is good. Don't forget it!*

I steal one more glance under the table
at your new wings breathing

across your calf—the ink alive
in the fluorescent lights of the diner.

Triple Foam

Go find a carwash. Not any carwash—the one next to Appleby's with triple foam. Buy the "Deluxe"—spot-free rinse, fire bath and ceramic hard-shell buff & shine. Now is not the time to cut corners. Approach the green light of the car wash entrance. The light flashes red, your car in neutral, feel the jolt of the conveyor engage. You cannot change where this is going.

Let go of the wheel—steering is useless. There is no clinical trial you have not explored, no drug that you have not researched for her. Turn on some music. Maybe Bob Marley, to remind you of beaches you walked together. Lean your head back against the headrest, close your eyes. The water pelting the roof hammers your sorrow into something leaden, yet small enough to fit in your pocket. People say that mourning a friend—unlike family—won't last. Carry your grief for as long as you must.

As the dense, gray strips beat the side of your car, forgive yourself for not coming sooner, staying longer, calling more often. Open your eyes for the triple foam. Remember how you drove through this car wash together after so many shifts together in the ER—when it was busy or it wasn't, when a patient died or they lived.

As the yellow, pink and blue foam rolls down your windshield, don't think of the day she was diagnosed ten years ago, when you sat together on a limestone bluff and watched the sun bleed orange into the sky behind Cheat Mountain. *Let the journey begin,* she said, as you hugged her. Choose another sunset. The one in Albuquerque where balloons lifted into the twilight: Dumbo and a pink hippo, Snoopy and Pac Man. Both of you quiet as the burners breathed life into nylon, the colors and stripes inhaling—each balloon a sunrise against the darkening sky.

Now is when you reach under the seat and open a Corona. Toast her, *To hot air, to triple foam, to our friendship.* The light is still red. Finish your beer. Tell yourself, *I have all the time in the world.*

Loam

How many times must experts
        remind me
you can't beat
        winter pansies
for color, but they
        wither
at temperatures over
        65 Fahrenheit?
If you want something
        that survives
all winter & comes back stronger—
        barrenwort carpets
your garden in green. Coreopsis is
        disease resistant;
insects don't care for the taste of
        their blooms.
Baptisia can live
        for decades;
several specimens survived
        since 1950
in the Better Homes and Gardens Test Gardens.

I fled from assisted living.
        to the plant section
at Lowe's, swapping
        Room 232,
its roll-in shower and call bell,
        for loamy pots
of orange mums, gold marigolds,

the same color as her suede recliner
        with a second-floor view
of the parking lot pansies.
        An incision
mounded her scalp. Her
        forehead flowered
pink from radiation.

Both of us wore
        Kmart shirts
bought ten years ago for a 60s party
        —fluorescent green daisies,
tangerine sunflowers—bodies
        sprouting neon
Room 232 was
        a greenhouse,
rows and rows of seedlings
        thriving,
our hug—a garden exploding.

Three Dreams After Your Brain Tumor Recurs

—for Erin, May 2025

1.

Watching the Strawberry Moon etch the black boundary between sand and sky with orange, I text you, as I did for decades. Remembering you can no longer read, I yell across three hundred miles—*Erin, full moon rising!*—certain you will hear me in your small room in assisted living, where the window is cracked. Then I see you—under the purple butterfly tree in the yard of the house you sold when you could no longer walk. Pink flipflops. Green Eagle's ballcap. Your face tipped towards the sky. Laugh like gravel. *Chinnis, I see it!*

2.

After your awful diagnosis of recurrence, you are feeling triumphant to have dined with death for two decades. Now, it's death who feels jilted. His bride, you will soon leave him tossing and turning alone in a clock's blue glow. Death exhausted—your revenge for his seven thousand three hundred nights of terror.

3.

We sit on a bluff at Cheat Mountain, sun bleeding into the river below. You pass me the leash with your mutt Bernice, who shudders as if shaking water from her fur. My hand goes up to my face to take off the rose-colored glasses you loaned me thirty years ago. To return them before you leave me. I feel nothing but eyeballs. "How will I see, without them?" I ask you. *Open your eyes,* you say. *The view is incomparable.*

August

—for Erin

How certain the lesser bittern, motionless
in this unlikely summer shower,

reading the rain-rippled creek
from the southern live oak's

fallen elbow. Silver shadows nibble
swamp grass, unaware of their fate

when the rain breaks—gill net,
gas spill, or gullet—as death,

ten years ago, tapped you
with a brain tumor. You taught

me long before that
what friendship is. Death,

impatient, spun you each month
in the MRI. Yesterday, on your scan

dense, muddy margins. On my dock, alone,
in this rain between June and September,

I am blindsided. Soon, I will lose you.
I still smell your cigarette, you

mouthing O's of smoke, laughing
at the rain's unlikely timing, scheming

how we can care better for our ER
patients. *Why don't you let them eat*

while they wait for the doctor? You,
always hungry for a hot pepperoni roll

and a cold Corona. I have treaded water
without you to this eddy

where a crab trap snares half
an oyster shell. The current swirls one

black osprey feather. May I cling
to your belly laugh: barnacle tethered

to piling. I have always known some life can't
survive in brackish water. May the oyster shell

embrace me in its pink and teal hollow. Forever,
may I hear you, laughing like sunrise.

Leaving

Where I visit you now,
sits on a hill rainbowed
by sassafras in October.
A one-lane road dead-ends
at Harmony Assisted Living.

Where I visit you now, the lobby
never misses a season: pumpkins
painted with black cat faces,
a candy-corn colored paper
taped to your door—
"Hospice Comfort Pack." Morphine,
Atropine, stool softener, Xanax.

I lean over your plaid
recliner to hug you, friend
of my heart, laughing into my hair.
I have met someone here. Timing
is everything. We eat Cheetos,
catch up on nieces, their babies.
I won't go through it again.
　　　　"Chemo, you mean?"

I remember hiking with you
in a forest of hornbeam,
asking, "What do you wish for your
fortieth birthday?" Tipping your face
to the twisted bark, the stubborn
orange—*Grace to face winter.*

My visit over, we crunch
deep-red leaves of the black gum
tree that muffle your walker's
scrape on the pavement. Determined
to walk me to my parking space,
to tell me good-bye. He calls
to you, limping past scarecrows
to place his hand over yours
and steady your walker as softly
as a sycamore peeling.

You wink at me, buttered leaves
of the white hickory tree
spilling around us.

Limbo

That's us in white, you—my bride—
and I, outside the Methodist church,
sandwiched between broomstick
and cut grass, backward bent
        in limbo.
Propelling liquid spine. A swift passing
under, one before the other, so close my breath
is leading yours, our fingers touching, easy
to arrive together, like a cold knife
to an apple's slice,
        almost simultaneous.
If only seconds matter to the slices.

If once, magnolia blooms won't curl.
If once, we can preserve enough figs
        for fall, fell one oak
warm enough to thaw the winter.
If we can sit holding hands
        on the dock by the creek,
        watch the last sunset.
If a color chart exists from which
        to paint a death together.

Here we are—my new knee, your
compression hose—crossing
over, slower, your hand reaching.
Bend a little lower, love. One last
shimmy under. Not this setting out
alone, in limbo.

Death

—after Anne Sexton, "Old"

I am tired of saying good-bye. I despise
        limping and tripping
up stairs. I dread waiting in hard,
        plastic chairs
for grim diagnoses, and now I know
        how death begins.
Like a poem blurred by my thick
        cat-eye glasses.
Like a hummingbird
        in my throat
when I hear my mother's
        laughter.
She plucks a yellow
        honeysuckle
from the rusty gate in Galena,
        pinches off
its stem, pulls the stamen
        through the bloom.

Open your mouth, she says to me.
Catch the honey with your tongue.

A Confusion of Senses

I am obsessed with the buzz
        of fluorescent lights in the ER.
At 5 a.m., it's so loud my hands
        can feel it—a sign my night shift
is almost over, unless a patient comes in
        dying—then clocking out
is a crapshoot. Is death like that—
        a sudden confusion of senses?
Your eyes hear goodbye, your ears
        see tears, your fingertips taste coffee
on the lips of your love, your nose
        is surprised by the sunrise
outside the ambulance doors.

I am older than the stethoscope
        my dead uncle gave me at my
med school graduation. Older
        than my mother's
Revlon *Cherries in the Snow*
        lipstick on my dresser. I am older
than my grandmother's silverware
        shoved under my bed. Maybe
we are forgotten like that. Metals
        tarnishing at different speeds. I am older
than the *Concise Roget's Thesaurus*
        my mother gave me in third grade
when I proclaimed verbs exultant.

I work another 24-hours & lose
another day. Forget six more words
to describe the ER's joy and sadness.
Several months later, I have mislaid
a paragraph. After forty years, I worry
I have nothing new
to write about suffering or healing.

I am older than the steel
of the scalpel I stole from work
to trim the stems from rainbow chard.
Older than penicillin. Older
than Hippocrates. I am older
than the great blue heron who landed
on my dock this morning. I have always
wanted to look graceful, effortless—
especially when dying. I watch
the heron, the S of her neck
not searching, but expecting, as if
it's 5 a.m. in the ER,
fluorescent lights buzzing.

About the Author

Ann Chinnis is the recipient of a Pushcart Prize (2025), two Best of the Net nominations, and a second-place Edgar Allan Poe Prize from the Poetry Society of Virginia. She authored two previous poetry chapbooks—*Poppet, My Poppet,* and *I Can Catch Anything*. Her work is published in *Sky Island Journal, River Heron Review, Gyroscope, Crab Creek Review,* and *The Orchards Poetry Journal,* among others. She studies at the Writers Studio with Philip Schultz. Ann is a retired Emergency Physician and a leadership coach, and she lives with her wife in Virginia Beach, Virginia.

www.ingramcontent.com/pod-product-compliance
Lightning Source LLC
LaVergne TN
LVHW090531110826
845146LV00003B/1061

* 9 7 9 8 9 0 1 4 6 9 7 9 8 *